BEHIND THE THIRSTY INSTINCT

MANGAL SING KRO

Made with ♥ on the Notion Press Platform
www.notionpress.com

To the readers...

Contents

Contents

Preface

The whole journey of the writing of this book is quite interesting. I started to write quotes to express my hidden thoughts. Later on, I added, modified and finally decided to make it in poetry form. The writings are very simple and completed in a short period. The subject matters included in the writings are mainly current socio-economic, polity, environmental issues and my nostalgic and raw childhood days. The social and economic inequality, exploitation of natural resources, competition for the show off life, changes I have seen in the environment, happiness in a small thing etc., are focused in the writings. In this writing journey, I would like to thank my beloved wife who always supports me in every aspect of my life.

Mangal Sing Kro

North Lakhimpur, 2022

1. 90's

I still remember the days
when the songs from Vividh Bharati
warm up the silence and cool morning.
When the darkness falls,
the sun hides amidst the night,
we take our dinner in the dim lights of the kerosene lamp.
The evening 8'O clock seems midnight,
the sounds of a flowing river and
the winds kissing the water
can be heard even from distance.
Every Friday night, we go two kilometers away
and watch Bollywood movies at 9.30.
The English and Hindi news explode
on the TV's screen before starting the movies,
still, I don't take away my two eyes off the screen,
as if, I understand everything.
When Sunday comes,
we rush to watch for Shaktimaan.
If the owners do not allow us in
we peep from the holes in doors and windows.

2. The Cowboy

When I take out the cattle
to graze nearby the Borkang river,
I often take rest under a tree
and sit leaning toward its trunk
to get relief from the weariness
in the sunny summer days.
The winds visit intermittently
to cool my heated body.
The white Kans flowers blooming
nearby the river
try to dance with the rhythms of the winds.
Sometimes, I drowsily lie down under the tree
letting the cattle rest in my surrounding.
The spotted doves often coo on the standing tree,
seem they look after the grazing cattle.
The mynas jump from one cow to another
seem to entertain them.
When the heat of the burning red sun
diminishes in the evening,
the cattle get ready to come back
to enter the cowshed.

3. River

When the earth was young,
I was always on cloud nine.
I could go anywhere I want
and I could stretch my arms
wherever I wish.
I could take breath freely
as nobody came to
grasp my neck tightly.
I bring up fishes
let them fly on my way,
I nurture plants
let them grow
to cool their neighbours.
I feel blue now
as you all have obstructed my way,
encroached the boundaries and
taking away fish.
You all are throwing wastes
on me, on my ways.
I want to prevent you
whenever you come to pollute me.
But, as you know

I cannot speak as you do,
I am helpless now.
Whenever the rain comes down
cats and dogs
I fail to accommodate them
to stay on way,
hence, I let them enter your houses.

4. Rice Field

The rice plants of our lands
grew under the assistance of the earthworms,
derived energies from the sun's rays,
invited different birds for the meetings
and arranged free lunches during the breaks.
They are now growing as usual,
eager to make themselves golden,
look for the rain,
but fail to understand
why earthworms are often absent
and less number of invited birds meet.

5. Competition

Everywhere in the world
has organized the competition of consumption,
and we are the participants to win the game.
We always try to raise our consumption,
buy a lot of unnecessary
to fill up inside our buildings.
We collect enormous properties in greed,
build skyscraper buildings,
look for costly branded,
throng to the crowded,
but, we forget to inhale the cool breeze,
couldn't see the beauty of the
morning diamond dews,
and fail to feel the happiness of
different birds chirping.

6. Life in Summer

The rain falls heavily from
the dark cloud-covered sky
entered into houses and
cast away the owners from their rooms.
The frogs who croak in the ponds
even climbed up to the roofs
to take shelter from the soaring water flows.
The cattle and goats grazing in the meadows
moved toward the highland
to save their own lives.
The cocks and the hens drowned in the water
as the angry water swallowed the coops.
The people dreaming to build their houses
rushed to the highlands
taking children on their shoulders.
The sound waves of the cries and screams
of children spread everywhere
as their throats dry up in thirst and fear.
The sunlight which showers the sweat
on the people in summer
was precious during a month-long rain.

7. The Ordinary Rose

Thousands of poets
make the rose a queen of flowers.
But, when I look at the blooming Bougainville
the rose fails to attract my two eyes.
When the fragrance of night jasmine
travels through the winding wind
and enter into my nostrils,
the fragrance of rose cannot touch
even the apex of my nose.
When the lotus blooms in a pond
and water lily stands beside her
by opening the veil from her face,
I take my eyes from the rose
and cast them towards the pond.
When the marigold and
the sunflower bloom
and take sunshine in the morning,
rose shyly hides under its veil.

8. The Darkness

I saw my neighbour trembling in the cold
as if a heavy earthquake was shaking him harshly.
He was covered with three thick blankets
still the cold was devouring him from head to toe.
A group of villagers like the swarm of flies
gathered around buzzing like bees.
Everyone was blaming the unseen deity of a river
that was flowing peacefully between the village
and poured water into their paddy fields.
Hundreds of villagers died from Malaria
but still, the deity of the river was blamed.
I saw people from remote areas
took sufferers in clothes
tied between the bamboo poles to the hospitals
like the hunters take animals to their homes.
They were obliged to come on the muddy road
in incessant rains
after crossing the angry river in the summer
when somebody falls sick.
Many villagers preferred to go to oracles
to know the causes of their illness
and many of them didn't go the hospitals

as they didn't know the language
to communicate with doctors and nurses.

9. Nature's Love

When the fire flames flare up in the sky
and sweat wets our body
you come to give shed and blow cool wind.
When heavy rain comes down from the cloud
and leads to the devastating flood
you come to rescue by your rays.
Everyone is trying to snatch your ornaments
you are still patiently protecting us.
People are greedy and ungrateful,
showing off and being hypocritical is their nature.
They take their needs and
spit back at you.
They remove your clothes and cut your arms,
they shave your hair and try to make it bald.
Your fleshes are removed from one place
and placed in other places.
I have seen you sobbing in sadness,
I have heard you shouting in a rage
still, you are patiently protecting us.

10. Hungry Elephants

Homeless elephants come to villages
in huge emotional pain,
perhaps, they try to ask for foods
in their languages
to drop inside their big empty stomachs.
They come in a herd,
shiver in hungry,
weep in grief,
tears fall down their cheeks
as their homes are lost amidst the villages.
They move from one village to another,
wander to find their ways,
ask people to give them space.
They are often lost amidst villages,
get bullied and harassment
from the inhabitants.

11. The Window

When the summer pours
warm water on my body
I open the window to
Welcome the light breeze,
and when the winter throws
cool dews on the green grasses
I open the window to
look at their glittering in
the morning golden sun rays.
The sounds of evening's noisy insects
try to enter through the window
when I close it at dusk.
The window which assists me
both summer and winter are now decaying,
the colours that I painted are
also disappearing.
Its woods are eaten away by the termites.
The time ticking to replace
with a new wooden frame,
but, how will I chop
the lone standing tree in my yard
as I haven't planted any trees yet.

12. The Lost

We leave for the cities
with the dresses, we wear in our villages
and leave behind the golden rice fields
along with the cattle
grazing in the meadows.
We leave behind the
the crowing of the cocks
to hear the roaring of the vehicles.
We leave behind the
the bleating of the goats
to hear the hubbubs of the people.
When we reach the cities,
we take off the dresses that
we use to wear in villages.
We walk as others walk
and talk like others talk.
When our children are asked
to speak in our mother tongue
they pretend to be others and
reply in cocktail languages.

13. Darkness in the Lights

Every year we long to embrace
the cool winter
after a long wait in the hot summer.
When the sitting dews on the grass
start to glitter in the morning sun rays
and the cool wind spreads the fragrance of
night flowering jasmine,
then the festival of light comes
and illuminates every part of the darkness.
The cities are climbed by the fairy lights,
the bursting and roaring of the
firecrackers in the sky
are like the blasting of the stars.
When the festival of light comes,
some villagers aloof from electric lights
even lit up Diya lights.

14. Extinction

The childhood I spent on the riverside is now
just a picture imprinted in my memory.
I often go to the riverside
to inhale the cool wind when I feel warm
and let the wind touch my naked skin.
When I dip my feet in the clear water of the river
in winter,
the chills enter my foot
and climb up through my veins.
When I look around the water,
I could feel the schools of fishes
celebrating the winter
after the harsh life in summer.
Now, the pictures of the river have changed,
people pour poison for fishing
and celebrate the winter in the river.

15. Change

The droplets of the hills create streams
are drying up slowly
as the peaks are filled with footprints.
The cool and silence of the surrounding are
erasing by the sun's heat slowly
as the trunks of the trees are sliding down
to the bottom of the hills.
The beauty of the hills is deforming slowly
with every heavy rain
as the protector trees are taking
by human beings.

16. Reminiscence

In the silence of new moon nights
when the fireflies lit up their lights,
the hungry frogs often crook in the ponds
look for the coward insects in the lights.
When the moon casts its full light
in the full moon nights
we often lay down on the bamboo mat
in our courtyard,
and count the scattered twinkling stars.
When we attentively listen
folk tales from my mother in the night,
the hen and the chicks even stay awake
to listen to them up.
And when the daylights start to erase
the darkness of the nights,
the cocks start crowing
to embrace the morning golden lights.

17. A Farmer's Joy

When the sprouts come out
after cracking the seeds
and shower themselves in the raindrops,
I feel thrilled and joyful.
In the early cool and foggy morning,
when the entire village is silent,
the mother birds embrace their chicks
with their wings to warm them up
and the cocks crow to wake us up,
I get up and cast
my two eyes towards the garden.
When the morning sun pours golden rays
and the dew sticking on the green buds
start to glitter,
then the breezes of happiness
flying around the garden
enter into my veins.

18. Destination of Equality

Everybody knows where
our final destination is,
still, we live in hope,
move ahead with dreams,
spend life in happiness and sorrow.
We flow in the waves of time,
cannot say who would reach earlier.
Our final destination might be
above the sky
where greed, longing, and pride
would disappear.
The emotions of desire and willingness
would be erased from our souls,
nobody would hold property
as the feeling of hungry won't exist.
Everybody would be equal.

19. Leaving Life Behind

We leave for a congested and crowded world,
leave the green village,
fresh water and clean air behind.
We run behind on costly clothes
finely decorated in giant shopping malls,
look for various restaurants foods,
and touch our hands on
the burning prices of our surroundings.
We live in small concrete rooms
which often boiled with
the scorching heat of the sun,
the water taps pour even warm murky water
seems they add fuel to fire during the summer.
When we step out from our boiling rooms
to cool down our burning brains,
We inhale dust particles along with the flying air.
The sounds of the vehicles continuously knock our ears
and the stinks often try to enter through our nostrils.

20. The Bongder

The place where the Bonder
grows and get ripens
invites many couples
to have a date in its surroundings.
The open place,
where the cool breezes come
rom the Borkang and Dikal rivers.
A few trees in between the shrubs
provides shade to
the romantic youngsters.
When they start to get ripen
people in love invite their loved ones
to visit the place
and promise to dance together
in the upcoming Chomangkan.
They get ripen in the season
when brainfever birds and cuckoos
exchange their words
and enjoy full happiness.

21. The Guards Wearing Green Clothes

The guards wearing green clothes
and standing in rows on the two sides of the roads
do greet and smile to every traveler,
give shades with their green shawls
in every winter, autumn, spring, and summer.
People take rest under their big arms
when they feel tired,
they make their food,
do not take any wages and salaries
even though they were appointed
to look after the people passing by.
They lean forward, backward and sideward
let their hair fly
when the winds pull and push them from every side.
But when the rulers planned to extend the roads
they were dismissed from their jobs
evicted from their places.

22. Behind the Thirsty Instinct

The life which is letting us live
will vanish away one day
like the sun sets in the evening.
Our lives would be lost somewhere
where nobody can see or touch them.
Life's clocks are ticking very fast
to reach their destinations,
still, we forget to live them.
Craving for competition and
greedy nature overcomes our natural way of living.
The hypocrisy which is creeping into our veins
forces us to hide our inner reflections.
The world where we compete
to keep our identity might turn lifeless
as we are thirstily sucking its blood always.

23. Tears of the Homeless

The sky caught fire in high flames in the summer
led to boiling between land and the sky,
the tree leaves longing to flip freely
were staying like statues
owing to the dearth of the winds.
One day, a group of monsters
like scorpions and crabs
entered into a village,
shook and wrecked the whole houses
which were built ten years back.
The place turned into hue and cry,
a bird sitting on the tree was
even shedding tears
as the standing tree sheltered them
might be cut down by the new builders.
The dogs felt afraid
as they might have to stay on the streets
when big buildings would replace
poor's tiny houses.

24. Helpless Lady

In the silence of midnight,
the moon and the twinkling stars
were locked by thick black clouds,
hefty incessant rain was pouring
from the black sky,
hence, a crowded East city was
flooded with angry water.
The rain had been pouring
a week and
black dirty water was
swallowing the house of
a helpless old lady
whose sons were building their
houses in the west's cities.

25. Joy in the Grass Roots

Everyone flows with time
and chooses different ways of life.
Some people climb the ladder to touch the sky
and roll their eyes over their subordinates
but fail to grasp the family members with their eye lenses.
Some people extract energies
from their bodies and souls for the entire year
and go far away to get peace once a year.
Some people gather enormous properties,
but let their lives flow like poor ones.
Some people spend money to show off in surroundings
but think twice to spend even for a cup of tea.
Some people do sacrifice their entire life
as their veins have flowed with the blood of particular belief.
Some people tie the plough with yoke,
hold in grip, walk along the bullocks
and whistle in an easy mood in tune.
Some people water the flowers,
look after the flower gardens
and joyously witnessing colourful butterflies
chasing around blooming flowers.

26. An Orphan Cuckoo

A naked thin tree standing in my yard
had started to wear new green leaves,
the twigs and branches were getting stronger
and forgetting their long sickness.
Diamond-like water drops were dropping from
the apex of leaves and flushing on the tops
of opening arum leaves.
When I look up at the fresh green crown
I saw a beautiful cuckoo sitting on a small branch.
He tried to sing their folk songs,
letting us know the spring season,
but the sound hardly came out of his mouth.
Perhaps, he didn't get a chance
to learn from his parents.
I saw a man roaming in the village
with a bag on his back and a catapult in his hand.
He was looking at the sitting cuckoo
who lonely tried to sing their songs.

27. Scary World

I feel scared sometimes in this world
where, love, emotion, and fraternity are left behind.
People run behind money by closing their eyes,
people run behind in popularity by covering
their faces with the white masks.
I feel scared sometime in this world
where truth & justice are often left behind.
People with power often kill the truth,
people with power often hide the truth.
I feel scared sometimes in this world
Where culprits freely roam under the shadow of someone
and the people sell their minds for a glass of wine.
I feel scared sometimes in this world
where greed and evil are swallowing human minds.

28. Happiness in Surrounding

I spent my childhood
amongst different chirping birds
whose sounds travel with pure air
and knock at my eardrums.
When the rain streams down from heaven,
the tailor birds start to rest
inside their dangling nests.
When the sun goes to sleep
in the bottom of the deep ocean in the evening,
mynas start to call their family members
to sleep in the bushes of bamboo trees.
The songs of brainfever birds during the spring
awake me up to pluck sweet and sour ripen fruit Bonder.
Sometimes, I did spend day long vacuum stomach
when our kitchen goes empty,
still, I could derive happiness from the surrounding.

29. From Forest to Villages

A small clean river was streaming
from the deep forest,
sieges of herons compete to catch
the freely swimming fishes.
I played with fish hooks
often nearby the hunting long neck white herons
and did come back with joy
after getting a few fish.
I had often seen wood logs loaded trucks
ever since I could open my eyes,
they used to come from the forest
and passed through my village.
I used to catch those running trucks
amidst the bursting smoky clouds of dust
and with my hard grip, I swung at their tails.
I didn't know the deep green forest
would transform into villages
and trucks would not have wood logs
to carry on their backs.
I didn't know
even the croaking frogs would be eaten away
and the herons wouldn't be seen catching fish.

30. Sorrow amidst the Happiness

A place circumambient with hills
where the cool wind waves the standing trees,
the slopes are dropping their hems with green leaves
and the soothing burbling sounds of streams
are pouring from the cols amidst different birds chirping.
People do come here from vehicle-flooded cities
for relaxing among the buzzing bees.
They return to their places
after recharging immense peaceful energies.
But I can feel the pains and cries of some poor inhabitants
amidst the beautiful surrounding.
People walk down far away
to exchange forest herbs with kerosene
to light up the lamps in the silence of nights.
With teary eyes, thousands of mothers
leave their young children miles away
in the hands of the unknown to do daily household chores
in exchange for their basic education.
I've seen people walk miles away amidst heavy rains
confronting thirsty bloodsucker leeches

on the narrow sloppy paths
to take their sick mothers to the hospital beds.

31. Tears of Wildlife

We're enjoying the greenery
to fill our endless wants
and exploiting the resources
until our eyes get tired.
Some people celebrate their freedom
and some are for their rights,
but who would come out for
the rights and freedom of
guiltless innocent wild animals and birds.
People are racing for their careers
and hence roaming every corner,
only wild birds and animals are always crying
for losing their family members.

32. Division

We'd broken the chain together
which was handcuffed by the colonizers,
dreamt to walk freely under the clear blue sky.
we'd promised to avoid the fight in the future,
we'd promised to enjoy together the beautiful nature.
We'd chosen our way, made our holy days,
but, addiction to holiness is reducing our friendliness.
we identify ourselves by the colour we wear
rather than the colour of our blood,
we identify ourselves by the colour of our skin
rather than our kin.
We fight for a silly thing
ignoring our long bonding,
we fight for a silly thing
but the benefits are grasped by the cunning kings.

33. Wooden Bed

We do make wooden beds and see our dreams
by laying down our heads on the pillows.
We add bunker-like boxes between the
side rails and the bottom side rails,
use additional pieces of wood
to make it look more glamorous.
We do make giant headboard slats
like the crown of the queens.
We do waste wood in making different shapes of
front and headboard legs, curve different
designs to show our artistic skills.
We love to make and buy luxurious beds
sometimes to show off our status,
love to spend our life with costly furniture
without planting any trees in our whole life.

34. Opportunist

We often feel perplexed
in this complex world,
unable to recognize even our own.
Our eyes often get blurred,
perhaps, we are often hypnotized
by some cunnings.
Whenever we do a friendship hug
they always stand between us,
wherever we do meet
they often divide us.
Everywhere is flooded with politics
and hence some people become opportunists.
Some people scream on the TV screens
to make the spectator confusing,
some people often loudly deliver the speech
just to make innocent foolish.

35. Changing Sceneries of Villages

The sceneries of villages have changed
in front of our eyes.
The chirping Mynas welcome the dawn
are hardly seen,
the nests of weaver birds
dangling from areca nut trees
swinging with the winds are also slowing disappearing,
perhaps, some thirsty cruel men are
mercilessly killing them catapults to suck their blood.
I still remember the horrific incident
when I was seven.
A group of people like restless monkeys
jumped from one tree to another
and grasped the innocent chicks from their shelter nests.
The helpless parents could
cry and scream only from far away.
The scenery of villages has changed
in front of our eyes.
The clean river flowing between the villages
are floating with the countless plastics

and the rivers are decorated with
smooth boulders become sandy.

36. Transformation

When I saw incalculable boulders
bedded along the Borkang river in my childhood days,
I used to think that
if these could have been eaten
I could have filled my empty stomach.
I often used to lick white substances
which stick with some boulders
as their taste was like salt.
I often threw stones at the river
just to count the steps of jumping on the water.
We took bath with friends nakedly
in the clear deep water,
swam like fish and made sand houses.
I had often seen nests of some birds
among the spreading boulders,
when we unknowingly go closer to their nests
they screamed and cried from distance.
Now, hundreds of trucks carry boulders
in a day from the river,
the river has started to flow above
the sands instead of the boulders
and the birds once happily played on the boulders

have disappeared from the places.

37. Diminishing

A river floating above the smooth boulders
was streaming between the hills,
the trees wearing green cloaks
which shadowed the flowing river
could also quench their thirst when they felt thirsty.
Fishes playing hide and seek in the bottom of
the crystal clear water was seen.
The hot winds crossing different cities
always turned into cool winds
when they mingled with the winds of the green hills.
When the door of winter starts open
my legs always step ahead to swim with the fish.
But, when I visited after ten years gap
I saw a drastic change.
Small fishes were even hardly seen.
I heard people do fishing by making electric shocks.
The greens were turning grey
and the sand was replacing the boulders.
Perhaps, the hills and the river have surrendered
in the hands of the people.

38. Blind

We're blind
living in this rich cultural world.
We couldn't see the beauty of diversity
which surrounds us.
We always try to see things
from our perspectives
and expect others to do the same.
We all are believing in Whatsapp University
ignoring our histories.
We couldn't see a group of hungry insects
slowly trimming away the pages of
the precious commandments.

39. Teary Eyes of the Earth

Our mother earth is crying.
Her teary eyes are telling us
of her deep pain.
Everyone is taking expenses
from her wrapped clothes,
still, nobody cares about her deep sufferings.
She warns us to take judiciously
to feed our future generations,
she requests us to apply ointment on her wounds,
but, we all are escaping from our roles.

40. Unhappy

We've come here for a few days
just to act on the stage.
We all know our lives
will be taken away,
still, we greedily gather properties every day.
We couldn't catch happiness
which is flying everywhere.
We're not ever satisfied
as we make ourselves hungry always.
We forget ourselves
where are we moving ahead,
we do struggle every day
just to enhance our nests.

Printed by Libri Plureos GmbH in Hamburg, Germany

9 798888 837047